D0742865

CALGARY PUBLIC LIBRARY

JAN   2009

M is for Mountie

An RCMP Alphabet

Written by Polly Horvath and Illustrated by Lorna Bennett

Thank you to the RCMP Archives, and the Glenbow Museum Archives
in Calgary, photo numbers: NA 1237-1, NA 354-1, and NA 17-5.

—Lorna

Sleeping Bear Press wishes to acknowledge Pete MacCormack,
Director of Licensing & Brand Management, The RCMP Foundation,
for assistance in providing resources and materials.

Text Copyright © 2008 Polly Horvath
Illustration Copyright © 2008 Lorna Bennett

All rights reserved. No part of this book may be reproduced in any manner
without the express written consent of the publisher, except in the case of brief
excerpts in critical reviews and articles. All inquiries should be addressed to:

Sleeping Bear Press™

310 North Main Street, Suite 300
Chelsea, MI 48118
www.sleepingbearpress.com

© 2008 Sleeping Bear Press is an imprint of Gale, a part of Cengage Learning.

Produced under License from the Mounted Police Foundation of RCMP © GRC

Printed and bound in China.

First Edition

10 9 8 7 6 5 4 3 2 1 (case)
10 9 8 7 6 5 4 3 2 1 (pbk)

Library of Congress Cataloging-in-Publication Data

Horvath, Polly.
M is for Mountie : an RCMP alphabet / written by Polly Horvath ;
illustrated by Lorna Bennett.
p. cm.
Summary: "The traditions, mission, and important work of the Royal Canadian
Mounted Police are explained using the alphabet format. Topics include badges,
investigation, Musical Ride, and rank. Poems are used to introduce each subject
accompanied by side-bar text filled with detailed text"—Provided by publisher.
ISBN 978-1-58536-267-7 (case)
ISBN 978-1-58536-451-0 (pbk)
1. Royal Canadian Mounted Police—Juvenile literature. 2. Alphabet
books—Juvenile literature. I. Bennett, Lorna, 1960- II. Title.
HV8157.H67 2008
363.28—dc22   2008009543

To Mary Wong

POLLY

*For Melody Jolane Scout, Cowboy Dave Manzer,
Garry Chaba, and Morris Crow—
in loving memory.*

LORNA

Aa

The title *Mountie* refers to a member of the Royal Canadian Mounted Police force (RCMP), which is the federal and national police force of Canada.

Most people think Hollywood came up with the saying, "The Mounties always get their man." Perhaps this is because of all the colourful Mounties that Hollywood has created over the years. But actually the phrase first appears in a report out of Fort Benton, Montana, in 1877 detailing an incident from Fort MacLeod in what is now Alberta. Captain William Winder and Major Acheson Gosford Irvine of the North-West Mounted Police (NWMP) captured three whiskey smugglers. The report went on to say that, although the Mounties lost their horses, "they fetch their men every time." This was later repeated and eventually evolved into "The Mounties always get their man."

There have been many famous fictional Mounties who helped create the romantic image of the Mountie who always got his man. They include "Dudley Do-Right" from the *Rocky and Bullwinkle* cartoon show, and Nelson Eddy and Howard Keel who were singing Mounties in the movie *Rose Marie*. Movie stars Randolph Scott, Robert Preston, Dick Powell, Tyrone Power, Robert Ryan, Donald Sutherland, Lee Marvin, and Peter O'Toole have all worn the famous red uniform and Stetson hat to play movie Mounties.

A is for "Always get their man"

This motto is an old one
and we certainly hope they do.
But let's be a little clearer:
They arrest their women, too.

The RCMP has many badges or insignia. The first badges appeared around 1876. They featured maple leaves, buffalo heads, a scroll with the title of the force, and St. Edward's Crown. Later the crown changed to reflect the reigning monarch of the time. Today that would be Queen Elizabeth II. Roughly translated, the motto written on the badge is *Maintiens le droit* or "Upholding the right."

There are many different kinds of badges. Just as guides and scouts wear sashes decorated with badges they have earned, there are RCMP badges showing special skills that have been mastered. There are skill badges for Musical Ride, Emergency Response Team, First Aid Instructor, Rough Rider, Dog Handler, Instructor, Forensic Identification Specialist, and Piper.

B is for Badges

Buffalo and maple leaves,
   Maintiens le droit, they read.
The badges of the officers
   express the Mounties' creed.

There are badges for service length: 5 years; 20-25 years; and 30-35 years. The most prestigious service badge is the RCMP Long Service Medal. It was approved by Royal Warrant and first issued in 1935. The medal is awarded to regular members of the force who have finished 20 years of good conduct and satisfactory service.

There are corps identity badges and a flying badge for those in air service. There are three appointment badges: Special Constable; Auxiliary; and Student. There are four sharpshooter badges and twelve badges denoting rank.

Depending on the dress, badges may be worn on the shoulders as slip-ons, or on shoulder boards or on the epaulettes.

C is for Cadet Training

Cadets are taught to see
from other points of view
when called upon in emergencies
to discover what is true.

Young adults (male and female) who train to become RCMP officers are called cadets. To apply to be a cadet you must be of good character, speak fluently in either French or English, be a Canadian citizen, have a high school diploma or equivalent, possess a valid driver's license, be 19 years of age at the time of engagement, meet medical standards, be willing to relocate anywhere in Canada, and be physically fit.

Cadets train at a special centre in Regina, Saskatchewan, called the Depot. In addition to meeting skills and educational requirements, cadets must also undergo extensive physical training. Their training can be quite rigorous with various exercises, including double-time marching, long runs, stair climbing, or weight lifting. RCMP officers must maintain their fitness levels. An officer may have to chase a criminal, climb a fence, or defend a victim of crime. He must be alert and ready for sudden action, which requires a fit body. Basic training runs for 24 weeks; upon graduation, cadets can be sent anywhere in Canada.

The RCMP believes in preventing trouble before it starts. The cadets are also taught to look at other people's points of view, an important tool in conflict resolution.

D is for Dale and Dogs

An officer can do the job.
It's never too big or tough.
And sometimes when he solves his crime,
the "officer" says *Woof*!

In 1933 Sergeant John N. Cawsey in Alberta used his German shepherd, Dale, to help him find a thief. Later, the judge presiding over the subsequent trial would not let the evidence that Dale had uncovered be used to convict the thief. In those days it was not established that a dog could assist in police work. But in 1935, after Dale had proved over and over that he was "top dog" at sniffing out crime, he became an official member of the RCMP. After that, a school in Innisfail, Alberta, was established to train dogs for use in police work. A breeding program was developed to produce dogs from Czechoslovakian working dog lines.

Puppies are tested at seven weeks to see if they will be suitable as police dogs. They are tested again at intervals after that, and those puppies not suitable are sold as pets. The rest are trained as police dogs.

Historically, the force trained its own sled dogs for use in the far north. Today the use of dogs has changed and now RCMP dogs have many different duties. A German shepherd's nose has more than 200 million scent cells (compared to the five million in humans). This makes them valuable for sniffing out lost children, drugs, weapons, and explosives. Dogs are also trained to be lowered from helicopters so they can work with Emergency Response Teams.

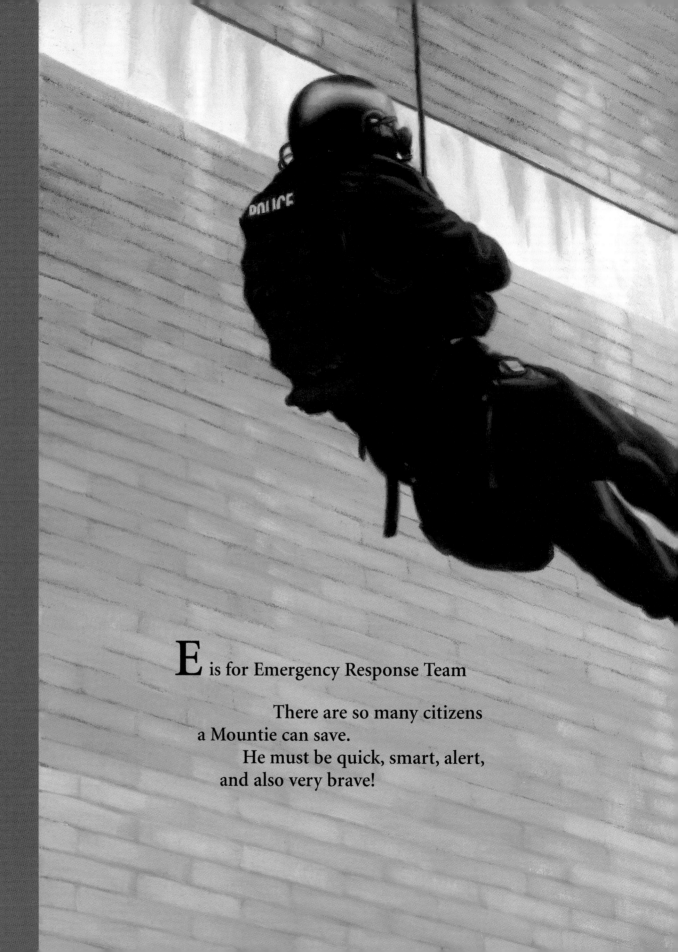

Mounties are all these things but sometimes even they need help. Who do they call? They call an Emergency Response Team (ERT), a group of specially trained RCMP officers who work together to handle dangerous situations.

The ERT program was established in the 1970s. Today there is at least one ERT in each province and territory in Canada. In addition to their regular police duties, ERT members participate in extra training and practice for emergency response work. Teams vary in size depending on their location and their special roles. Working with the teams are other specialists such as police dog handlers and crisis negotiators. These men and women must learn special skills, such as rappelling (climbing down the outside of a cliff or building while suspended from a rope).

An ERT is called in to handle dangerous situations where extra training is needed. For instance, a team might be called in to raid a ship suspected of carrying drugs. This requires special tactics and equipment that regular police officers do not have the training to use. In 2005 the Canadian government created a Marine Emergency Response Team. RCMP officers work with the Canadian Coast Guard on patrol boats in the Great Lakes St. Lawrence Seaway region.

E e

E is for Emergency Response Team

There are so many citizens
a Mountie can save.
He must be quick, smart, alert,
and also very brave!

F f

Not everyone knows that the RCMP has an air services branch with one of the largest fleets of aircraft in Canada.

The fleet began in April 1937 with four twin-engine biplanes and eight pilots. During World War II this fleet was down to just one plane, as the air force required the use of the other planes. After the war more planes were added, and in 1971 the fleet got its first helicopter.

In order to make sure that the fleet is "evergreen" (in tiptop shape and using the most current technology), an aircraft is retired after seven years of service and replaced with the latest version. The most important plane in the fleet is the single-engine seven-passenger Pilatus PC-12. The fleet also includes helicopters (most of which are replaced every 15 years) and floatplanes to land on water.

Aircraft in the RCMP air services branch are used for search and rescue operations to help Mounties working on the ground find people who have become lost in Canada's great wilderness areas. The planes patrol and also transport prisoners and supplies.

F is for Fleet

We know the Mounties ride their steeds,
drive cars, steer boats to do good deeds.
But sometimes crimes are seen on high
because the Mounties also fly.

How can you determine who is guilty of a crime if the criminal has disappeared from the crime scene? From the clues left behind, of course! But understanding what those clues are and how to look for them is a tricky business. That is why the RCMP has Forensic Science and Identification Specialists.

These specialists are the first officers to examine a crime scene. They wear rubber gloves and overalls called "bunny suits" so they don't contaminate a crime scene by leaving fingerprints or traces of their own! The specialists put evidence in bags and bring it back to their forensic labs.

There they have many special techniques to find, analyze, and interpret clues. For instance, by using certain chemical processes, they can make invisible finger-prints visible under ultraviolet light.

G g

G is for Guilty or Innocent

Fingerprints and fibres
and footprints are a few
of what an I.D. expert
can tell you make a clue.

H is for History

Canada's West
would need more forces
so Sir John A. Macdonald
put police on horses.

In the 1870s whiskey traders entered the regions now known as Alberta, Manitoba, and Saskatchewan. This created problems for the Hudson Bay Company, which had been trading with the natives for fur.

Sir John A. Macdonald, Canada's first prime minister, knew that settlers would soon arrive in the Canadian West, as they had in the American West. He wanted to have some kind of western law enforcement in place before then. He envisioned an organization along the lines of a military force to keep the peace. Following the common practice of mounted regiments in the military (and also because of the geography), it was determined members would be mounted on horses. This force became the North-West Mounted Police (NWMP). In 1920 the name was changed to the Royal Canadian Mounted Police.

These are rules from the NWMP's early years:

- Always be honest.
- Take proper care of your horse. Make sure it is locked in the stable at night.
- Always respect the members of your community.
- Put your pillbox hat* in a safe place before you go to sleep.

*The more familiar Stetson seen in dress uniform today later replaced this hat.

In G is for Guilty, you read about the Forensic Science and Identification specialists and how they collect clues. But what happens after that? The RCMP has forensic labs in Halifax, Ottawa, Winnipeg, Regina, Edmonton, and Vancouver.

These labs are where scientists use their expert talents to interpret the clues that are found. For instance, bullets left at the scene of a crime are tested in the firearms section to identify the kind of gun used. There are different sections within the labs to examine evidence: Biology Services; National Anti-Counterfeiting Bureau; Trace Evidence; Toxicology Services; and Firearms. A section called Forensic Imaging Services is located in Ottawa.

The firearms section has a wall featuring some of the different illegal weapons officers have taken away from criminals. Officers are shown these so they can learn about the types of weapons they might encounter on the street.

I i

I is for further Investigation

You may just wonder what those "guys"
who investigate with searching eyes
do with clues they happen to nab.
Well, of course, they send them to the lab!

Jj

There are many career opportunities in the RCMP. Once a cadet leaves the Depot, he or she may be posted anywhere in Canada. After three years of normal police duties, an officer is free to pursue a specialized field such as marine services, air services, crime prevention, federal policing, customs and excise, or passport and immigration. Perhaps the officer would like to be part of an ERT group or go into traffic law enforcement or airport security. Maybe he prefers the detection of counterfeit money or working in a lab. A dog lover might become a dog handler. Or maybe the officer will recruit or train other officers.

However, just because someone works for the RCMP does not necessarily mean being a Mountie. There are many ways to work within this organization while remaining a civilian member. The RCMP uses the services of psychologists, doctors, administrative assistants, and others. There is also a volunteer police force made up of civilians who are given special training to be auxiliary constables. Its members do not wear the yellow band seen on the hats of regular RCMP constables. Still, they are trained to do things like direct traffic, handle prisoners, and assist the regular constables.

Whether it is lab work or crime prevention, air services or passport and immigration, there is a job for everyone.

J is for Jobs

There are many ways to serve the force.
With planes and boats, on foot, of course,
in labs, or even to the source,
when Mounties first appeared on horse.

K is for Klondike

The Yukon was a region
where fortune favoured the bold.
Here Mounties came to keep an eye
on miners seeking gold.

One of the most satisfyingly successful RCMP operations was the peaceful establishment of a police presence during the Klondike Gold Rush.

The Yukon Territory covers 483,450 square kilometres (300,902 miles). Before 1886 primarily native people had settled the Yukon. When gold was discovered that year on the Fortymile River, hundreds of people came to seek their fortunes. The climate was brutal—from 36.1° C (96.8° F) in the summer to -60° C (-76° F) in the winter.

With the arrival of the first prospectors, the NWMP realized they needed to send a detachment to establish order before more arrived. They wanted to make sure it was understood that this area was Canadian and under Canadian law. Because of this foresight, when the gold rush later began in earnest with hundreds of prospectors pouring into the Klondike region, the Mounties were prepared. The gold rush was handled in an orderly, lawful fashion.

The gold rush has been romanticized and often written about. Jack London (his books include *Call of the Wild* and *White Fang*) took part in the gold rush. Poet/writer Robert William Service (whose cabin still exists in Dawson City) wrote of the gold rush and the wildness of the times.

Kk

L is for Legends

Men and women officers,
early wilderness wives,
horses, dogs, and constables
have all led storied lives.

Perhaps the most famous Mountie is Sam Benfield Steele. Steele joined the NWMP in 1873. He lived in the west during a time of great tumult, working to keep peace between the natives and white settlers. During the construction of the Canadian Pacific Railway, he even rose from a sickbed to avert a confrontation between striking workers and those who came to take over their jobs. Later Steele was sent to the Kootenay to quell tensions between natives and settlers, and then on to the Klondike during the gold rush. Throughout his long career Steele served in a variety of roles, including policeman and magistrate.

There are many legends among those who served the RCMP, including the wives. In the early days of the force, women were celebrated chiefly as officers' wives; however, since many lived with their husbands in remote wilderness locations, they also had to endure some of the same hardships.

Even the horses have their legendary characters. Part of the Musical Ride for a number of years, Lucky II was a versatile horse, able to perform any of the positions. He was chosen to compete in a police horse competition where he took first prize. Lucky II died at the age of 29.

L1

The first public performance of the Musical Ride was in 1887. The NWMP began the tradition to show off their riding skills and entertain local communities. Now the Musical Ride entertains people all over the world.

All the riders in the Musical Ride are police officers who have had at least two years of active police work. Some have never ridden a horse until they volunteer for this job. The members spend six months learning to ride and then are only allowed to perform in the Musical Ride for three years; this ensures that everyone has a chance to participate. The RCMP actually prefers officers who have *not* ridden before to those who have. It is thought it is easier to learn these skills new than to have to lose bad habits.

The RCMP breeds its own black horses for the Ride. Thoroughbreds were the horses first used, but in 1989 black Hanoverian broodmares and stallions were introduced to improve the stock's colour, substance, and conformation.

M
m

M is for Musical Ride

Famous, those horses! Their colour is black!
They carry police 'round the globe and then back.
They ride in formations, the "dome" and "wagon wheel,"
and with lowered lances, they charge with great zeal!

All the foals born in a given year are assigned names that begin with the same letter of the alphabet. The following year, names would begin with the next letter (except for Q, U, X, Y, and Z, which are not used).

It takes two and a half years to train a horse. The horses must be very calm and patient. Not only do they move to music and gallop in formation, these horses must also be able to travel well, march in parades, and stand still for petting and photos.

There are 32 horses and riders, plus a member in charge, in the Ride. They perform intricate figures, many of which are taken from old cavalry drills. They must be able to do these to music during the 40-50 events each year that they perform.

One of the most famous drills is the "Dome," which used to be featured on the back of the Canadian $50 bill. The "Charge" is probably the favourite of the drills, when riders lower their lances and charge forward together at full gallop. The finale is the "March Past" when the regimental march is played and the riders salute a guest of honour.

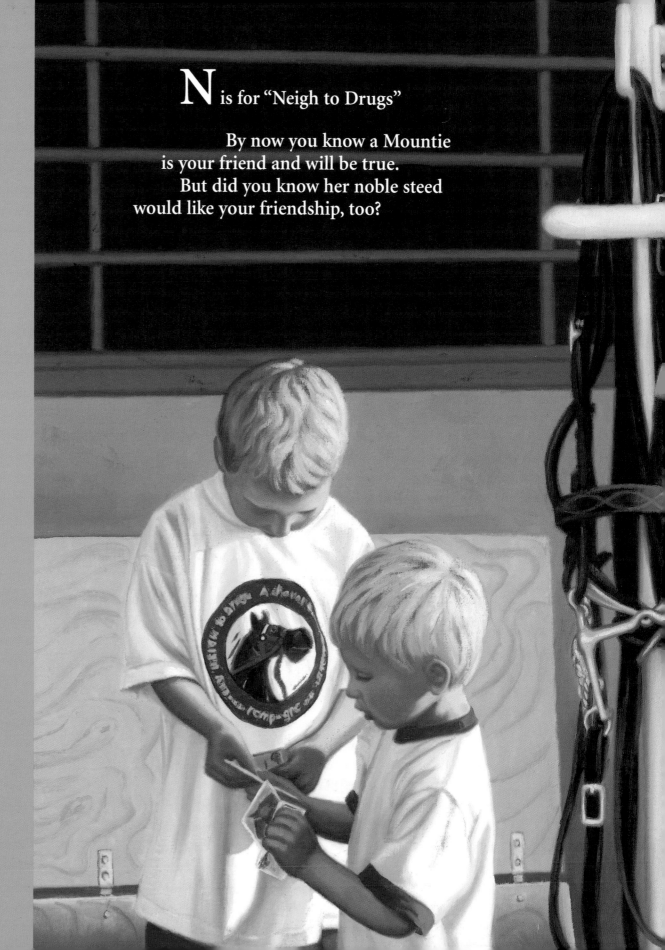

N is for "Neigh to Drugs"

By now you know a Mountie
is your friend and will be true.
But did you know her noble steed
would like your friendship, too?

The Musical Ride created a national drug awareness program to teach children and preteens about drugs and help them "Say neigh to drugs."

Members of the Musical Ride bring the program to communities. School talks, brochures, stickers, posters, pins, tattoos, and a cartoon horse named "Steele" help spread the message "Say neigh to drugs" in a fun and friendly way. The program encourages schools to run essay and art contests. Student winners can have their work published in the local paper or might receive a special tour of the Musical Ride horse stables to meet the officers and horses.

The RCMP has other programs to help children who might be at risk of turning to crime and guide them in making better choices. The officers go into schools to teach about bullying, drugs, responsible Internet use, and safety, among other things.

The position of operator is a very important one in the RCMP.

If you are in trouble, you may be quite excited when you telephone the RCMP for assistance. It is an operator's job to calm you down and swiftly get the necessary information in order to find just the right kind of help for you. An operator must be calm and able to think clearly in order to find out, for instance, your location, how desperate the situation is, and what type of assistance you need.

To help safeguard an officer out on call, an operator will monitor the officer's movements. Sometimes an officer calls the operator for information about a suspect. The operator will use a computer to get information from the Canadian Police Information Centre. Perhaps the suspect isn't Canadian. In that case the operator has to contact Interpol, an international police organization. An operator must be knowledgeable about all aspects of the RCMP.

O is for Operator

There are many ways to serve the force:
A Mountie can't do all, of course.
But if you're in trouble, best of all
is the person there to take your call.

Oo

P is for Jerry Potts

There're many who helped the mounted police,
and many who'd like to, no doubt.
But one of the early famous ones was
a Métis interpreter and scout.

Jerry Potts was well known among the early NWMP as an interpreter and scout.

In the early days of the NWMP, the force was establishing forts and beginning to police the North-West territories, patrolling for horse thieves and whiskey traders. Commissioner George Arthur French was looking for someone who spoke both English and native languages to help Assistant Commissioner James Macleod and his men find whiskey traders in the far west. Jerry Potts, a Métis who spoke both languages, was hired for the job. Together Macleod and Potts travelled to Fort Whoop Up (in what is now Alberta) to stop the whiskey trading but the traders had fled. The members of the NWMP went on to establish its first outpost in the west, naming it Fort Macleod.

Famous for being a good scout, Potts guided the NWMP safely through terrible blizzards even when he was snow-blind. He was also famous for making very brief interpretations. Once, when a native chief made a 90-minute speech to a visiting dignitary, Potts interpreted the entire speech as, "He wants grub."

Although he was not an official member of the NWMP, Potts was buried with full military honours when he died.

Queen Elizabeth II is not just Queen of England; since Canada is a commonwealth country, she is Queen of Canada as well. When she comes to Canada a division of the Mounties is assigned to protect her. One year Canada gave the Queen a special and unusual gift.

Burmese, a black mare born in 1962, was at first considered too small to be used in the formal Musical Ride; she was used instead to train the riders. She eventually grew to full size and was given a part in the Ride. Beloved by the members, she eventually outperformed all the other horses!

The RCMP decided to present the Queen with Burmese as a gift and in 1969 brought the horse to England. The Queen wanted to see Burmese perform one last time in the Musical Ride. The riders were nervous. Would Burmese do well in England in front of so many people? She performed perfectly. The Queen rode Burmese for the first time in the parade celebrating her 43rd birthday. And she continued to ride her over the next 18 years. After that, Burmese was put to pasture outside Windsor Castle where the Queen could visit her. After Burmese died, a statue was erected of the Queen riding her. Not bad for a horse that was once considered too small.

Q is for Queen

If someone said you could be queen,
    you might say, "Aw, baloney!"
But would you take the job if they
    would promise you a pony?

Rr

A cadet begins his training,
    lots of work and then some more.
But when it is all over,
    he can rise up through the corps.

A rank means a job in order of importance. Every new RCMP officer starts at the lowest level, Constable. He must be a constable for seven years until he can be promoted to Corporal. After that he can rise in rank, one rank per two years served. The ranks up until Inspector are noncommissioned officers. After this they become commissioned officers. The Canadian House of Commons must appoint commissioned officers. We use the term "officer" out of respect for all policemen, but technically only those who have achieved the rank of Inspector or above are officers.

Every police department has a group of constables on duty. These groups of constables are called watches. Every watch has a watch commander. A small community might have seven constables, with a corporal working as the watch commander. A large community might have 20 constables, a corporal, a sergeant, and an inspector acting as the watch commander. This is the order of the ranks:

Constable
Corporal
Sergeant
Staff Sergeant
Sergeant Major
Inspector
Superintendent
Chief Superintendent
Assistant Commissioner
Deputy Commissioner
Commissioner

An officer in the RCMP may start his career as a Constable, but he can work his way up to Commissioner, the highest rank, some day. Each rank has its own badge.

S is for the *St. Roch*

Mounties fight crime day or night,
by plane or car or horse.
The *St. Roch* cut through ice and seas,
patrolling far up north.

Around the beginning of the twentieth century several countries became interested in the arctic islands around the North Pole. At that time, explorers from Norway and Denmark tried to claim those islands for their countries. The Canadian government decided it must send Mounties north to live on Baffin and Ellesmere Islands so everyone would know those islands belonged to Canada. In 1928 the officers were joined by a patrol ship, the *St. Roch*. Built especially for the RCMP, the *St. Roch* (pronounced "Saint Rock") brought supplies up north but it also made the voyages to establish Canada's sovereignty on the islands and the Northwest Passage.

The *St. Roch* was built in 1928 in Vancouver, British Columbia. She was named after a parish in the Quebec city constituency then responsible for the RCMP. Because she was to travel the dangerous, icy Northwest Passage, her outer hull was built with thick Douglas fir and the very hard "iron bark" Australian gumwood. The inside was reinforced with heavy beams to withstand ice pressure. The *St. Roch* is 31.78 metres long (104.25 feet).

The *St. Roch* was able to handle the rough seas and could withstand the arctic winter. It was the first ship to get successfully through the Northwest Passage from west to east. It was also the first ship to circumnavigate North America. The *St. Roch* was retired after 20 years of service and is now in the Vancouver Maritime Museum.

T is for Tartan

Families have tartans.
The Scottish have many.
But did you know
that Canada had any?

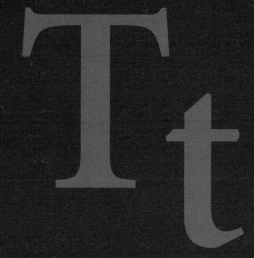

Well, it does. The RCMP has its own tartan. A tartan is a special plaid that belongs to a family or organization, and no one else may claim it for their own.

As in much of Great Britain, bagpipers in Canada have represented the RCMP at regimental weddings, funerals, parades, and ceremonial occasions for one hundred years. Many people felt that these pipers should be kilted in a special RCMP tartan so that it would be clear whom they were representing.

For many years there was talk about creating a tartan but it was the 1997 celebration of the RCMP's 125th anniversary that inspired a committee to finally do so. The wife of a former RCMP commanding officer designed a special tartan. It uses colours that have meaning for the organization.

The colour blue represents the uniform's traditional breeches. Scarlet is for the tunic. Yellow represents the cavalry stripe on the pants legs and the headband, along with the gilt of the badge. Brown is for the buffalo that roamed the prairies when the NWMP was formed. Green is for the Canadian maple leaf. White is for the lanyard and sky blue represents the hat colour of the Canadian peacekeepers. All these colours make up the special tartan that was formally presented by Her Royal Highness Princess Anne in June 1998.

All over the world a Mountie is recognized by the bright red uniform and distinctive Stetson hat.

The red uniform was first worn when the NWMP was formed back in the days when settlers were coming to Saskatchewan. The Canadian government wanted its policemen on the prairies to be easily distinguished from the Americans. The red coat has always been a sign of the British army and because Canada is a commonwealth country, the government thought this would be a good colour. Officers wore many different styles of tunic initially, as they were outfitted from militia stores and had to wear what was available. In time, one tunic style was selected.

The uniforms changed many times over the years. The NWMP wore grey or tan pants and shiny black boots when they were marching (for everyday use they wore brown boots). Originally they wore pillbox hats that were held on with chinstraps. Sometimes they wore helmets with feather plumes. The ranks were differentiated with different coloured plumes. The Stetson hat was gradually introduced as it was more suitable to police duties and the western terrain. In 1904 the force received the designation of "Royal," and blue facings were added to the uniform.

U is for Uniform

The Mountie is dressed in a bright scarlet red.
The boots are shiny, a Stetson on head.
All tidy and neat—with badges just so,
this uniform's known wherever you go.

In the early years sidearms were not worn, but today they are standard. Even the uniform belts have changed over the years from the original crossbelts to the brown Sam Browne-style belt worn today.

Today RCMP officers have dress uniforms and everyday uniforms. The everyday uniform consists of ankle patrol boots, a policeman's cap, grey shirt, blue tie, and blue pants with gold strapping. But there are many variations to meet various climate needs and to denote rank. For instance, short-sleeved shirts without ties are worn in the summer. Noncommissioned officers wear blue gorget patches on their collars, while commissioned officers have solid blue collars and blue pointed cuffs on their shirts.

The uniform must serve its members' needs. Those in the north wear fur hats, for example. A dog handler has a particular uniform and so does a peacekeeper. In 1990 Sikh members were granted permission to wear the turban instead of the traditional Stetson. It was decided that Sikhs were to be granted this special dispensation for religious purposes.

All officers must carry their metal badges on their person as part of their uniform. They do not wear them but rather keep them in a pocket or other convenient place. When officers retire, they may keep their badge and display it. A family member may inherit a badge but if they wish to keep it, it must be encased in plastic so that no one can use a badge to impersonate an officer.

V is for Village and Volunteers

The model village is where Mounties make
arrests that are just practice and fake.
There Mounties will give very stern looks
to volunteers who pretend to be crooks.

The RCMP's famous Depot Division or Training Academy is located in Regina, Saskatchewan. Both men and women live in dorms there, learning to become members. They are put into groups of 24, which are called troops. The cadets, as the students are called, must learn to prepare a search warrant, practice making arrests and testifying in court, and much more.

The cadets spend time practicing scenarios at an RCMP model village. The village has stores and banks and a courtroom, and various businesses such as you would find in a real town. But this one is all pretend. Volunteers from Regina help the cadets by playing different roles. For instance, they might pretend to be criminals robbing the hotel, or perhaps act as judges, lawyers, and jury members in a courtroom. By play-acting with these volunteers, cadets get to practice their new skills.

The Depot is quite a tourist attraction. Many people visit it every year. It houses the RCMP Heritage Centre, and in the summer evenings there are sunset full dress parades, complete with a flag-lowering ceremony.

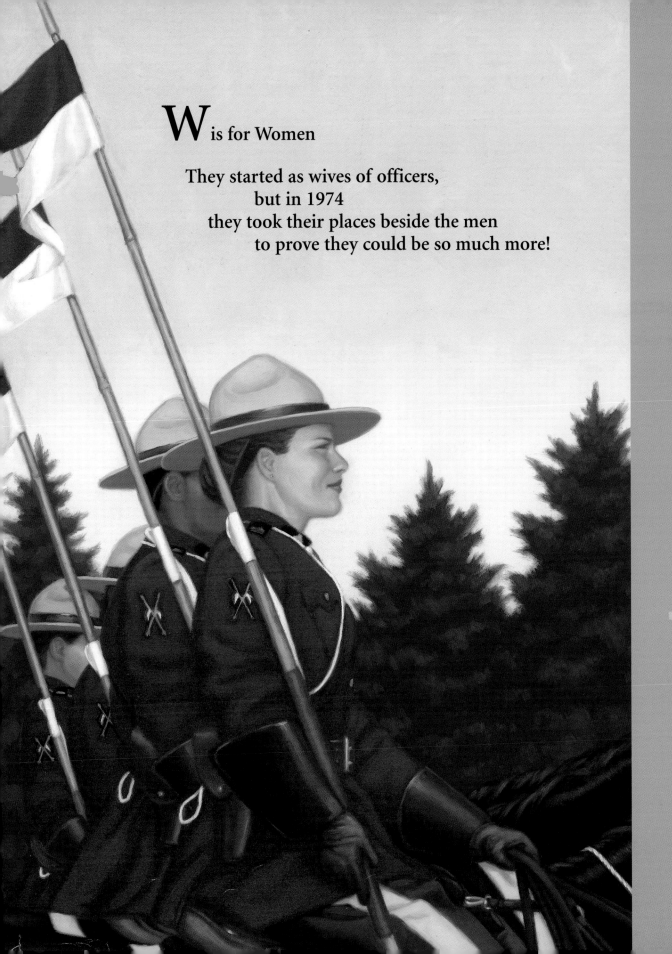

W is for Women

They started as wives of officers,
but in 1974
they took their places beside the men
to prove they could be so much more!

In the early days of the RCMP women were frequently hailed as courageous partners of the officers, posted in wild and remote places. Later they held jobs as technicians and female jailers.

Dr. Francis McGill is often called the first woman Mountie. She was a brilliant doctor and in 1946 was made an Honourary Surgeon at the RCMP laboratory in Regina. She was also a lecturer in forensic medicine at the training academy. During her career Dr. McGill helped solve many murders, travelling by float-plane, dog team, and snowmobile to interpret evidence in cases. When she died at the age of 81, the province of Saskatchewan named McGill Lake after her.

It wasn't until 1974 that the first troop (Troop 17) of 32 female regular members was formed and women became officers in their own right. Now women do the same jobs that the men do including, of course, riding in the Musical Ride.

W
W

The Hope Statue was created to mark Lloydminster City's 100 years and the 130th anniversary of the RCMP.

Retired RCMP veteran Glenn Wood coordinated the RCMP Veterans Association and the RCMP in the project. Rudi Schmidt, an artist and sculptor from Wainwright, Alberta, created the statue.

The Hope Statue is a large bronze. It depicts a Mountie in traditional uniform on bended knee, holding his Stetson in one hand. His other hand rests on the back of a child who is crying. At their feet is an injured dog. At the base of the statue, the word HOPE is spelled out in gold letters, along with the Canadian flag. On the sides of the statue are the words carefully chosen to represent what the RCMP means to the community: Respect, Family, Community, Freedom.

X marks the spot of the Hope Statue

The statue here is rightly named; it stands for many things—
For community and freedom and all that order brings.
For family and respect, for people living free,
for hope, and for a law force that's the best that it can be.

HOPE

Y is for Yukon Dempster Highway

Do you like long car trips
over snow?
Try a dogsled
at forty below!

Yy

The Yukon Dempster Highway is named after William John Duncan Dempster. As an RCMP corporal he was called "The Iron Man of the Trail" for his dogsled journeys between Dawson City and Fort McPherson (a 764-km trip, often in -40° temperatures) in order to patrol the region.

Dempster is perhaps best known for his role in the Yukon's famous "Lost Patrol" incident. In 1911 four members set out on this difficult patrol. In order to make the sleds lighter and faster, they decided to take less food. After 19 days out, the patrol missed a turn and became lost. Plagued by perilous cold and dwindling food supplies, they decided to turn back. Sadly, all four men eventually died before reaching Fort McPherson. When it was clear the patrol was overdue, Dempster led a party out into hazardous weather. They found the men's bodies in the huge greatness of the Yukon wilderness. Dempster's journals of this search became part of northern police history.

The highway follows Dempster's old trail, which he learned from the Gwitchin natives who learned it from their ancestors. It connects Dawson City in the Yukon to Inuvik in the Northwest Territories.

The RCMP doesn't just keep the peace in Canada; sometimes its officers act as peacekeepers in other parts of the world.

When two countries are in conflict, someone neutral is often needed to act as "policeman" to ensure that everyone is treated fairly. These "policemen" are called peacekeepers. The area that the peacekeepers patrol is called a demilitarized zone.

Since 1989, when the RCMP instituted its International Peace Operations Branch, they have sent over 2,000 peacekeepers to various missions around the world. The RCMP sends peacekeepers to do various things: They might help families whose houses have been destroyed by war or keep an eye on elections. They are there to help countries until they are able to operate on their own again. Peacekeepers have been sent to many places including Namibia, Haiti, Rwanda, Guatemala, Kosovo, East Timor, Guinea, Afghanistan, Jordan, and Iraq.

Z is for Peace Zone

The United Nations is working for peace,
which everyone wants in their heart.
By sending in officers specially trained,
Canadians do their part.

Zz

Fun Facts

There are a lot of interesting facts to learn about the Royal Canadian Mounted Police. Here are just a few. For instance…

Did you know…

…that the son of English author Charles Dickens was a member of the North-West Mounted Police?

…that the last dogsled patrol was in 1969?

…that horses in the Musical Ride need new shoes every six to eight weeks?

…that, similar to baseball cards, you can get Mountie trading cards?

…that the RCMP is unique in the world since it is a national, federal, provincial, and municipal policing body?

Helping to make a difference!

Established in 1994, the RCMP Foundation is a not-for-profit organization that manages the commercial use of the RCMP's image and protected marks through the RCMP Licensing Program. The proceeds from this program have contributed significantly to community initiatives across Canada in areas such as drug awareness, youth programs, crime prevention, victim services, and Internet safety.

For more information on the RCMP Foundation please visit www.rcmp-f.ca.

The responsibility for the historical accuracy of both the text and artwork in this book belong solely to the author and illustrator and not to the RCMP Intellectual Property Office. You are encouraged to learn more about the RCMP at http://www.rcmp-grc.gc.ca.